Maximize

your Investment

Returns

11 Questions
for your Advisors

Ian Sender
Former Director, Wall Street firm

IAN Books

An IAN Books paperback

Published by
IAN Books
41 Watchung Plaza, B242
Montclair, NJ 07042

Copyright © 2013 IAN Books

Cover photo: Businesswoman and office workers by <u>Victor1558</u>

Special sales for educational use by nonprofits.
<u>IANBooksEditor@yahoo.com</u>

ISBN-13: 978-1492193722

ISBN-10: 1492193720

Library of Congress Control Number: 2013948323

IAN Books at <u>Amazon.com</u>

Wealth Without Wall Street:
Buy Direct -- Avoid the Commissions, Fees, Loads

The Insiders' Guides to Buying Discount Financial Services:
Buy Direct and Save $3,000 Every Year

Drop Your Insurance:
Buy Only What You Need

Create Financial Freedom Using Your Wealth Reserve™:
Fix your financial life

The Simple Financial Life:
How to get what you want without going into debt and living
paycheck to paycheck

Build Wealth Without Extra Money or Time:
You don't need to budget or get an extra job

Leah's Money Book:
"I want to control my own money."

The Working Millionaire:
$2,000,000 Tax-FREE Wealth Reserve ™ Self-insure Self-fund

Build Your Own $2,000,000 Tax-FREE Wealth Reserve™:
Self-insure Self-fund your lifestyle

Stop wasting $3,000 every year:
101
financial products ***NOT*** to buy and why

Wealth:
What every high school graduate needs to know in the 21st century

Contents

Introduction

Very few advisors can beat the market returns over time
"In every period, low-cost funds beat high-cost funds"
Last year's genius is usually this year's idiot
Advisors can't predict future returns over time
Advisors want to attract short-term money for current profits

I have been in the financial services business for over 20 years. Commoditization has come to the financial advice business. Unless you have millions of dollars to let an experienced Registered Investment Advisors (RIA) build on, you are going to overpay for advice that can't beat the markets over time.

    The key question is what is your timeline. Are you investing to get rich quickly or are you investing to retire with $1 million in about 35 years? No legitimate RIA can promise the first goal yet many "professional" advisors imply that their work will make you wealthy. They don't mention a timeline.

    The fact is that *over time*, very few advisors have beaten the stock market returns that average 10-12% a year. As you know, there is no way to know which advisors will succeed in the future.

    So, **how can we maximize our investment returns** over time?

    Some of us have decided to go the "do-it-yourself" route. We figure that since an advisor can't beat 'em, we'll join 'em. We join with others as owners of shares of a market index fund. This mutual fund owns the same stocks as a market index that represents a good sample of all stock companies.

    Others have already been using an advisor and believe that it is better to let this person worry about the ups and downs of the markets. They are willing to pay 1-3% for this "hand-holding" process. They are willing to pay for the costs of trading and the taxes that result from buying and selling even if they earn less.

    What may not be known about using an advisor is how to evaluate their products—investment strategies and securities. We have to remember that we are buying a service and products when we pay an advisor. When we shop for investments, we are smart to remember the wisdom of Benjamin Graham, a mentor to Warren Buffett. Graham said,

"buy financial products like you buy "groceries, ... not perfume."

Graham was interested in getting his money's worth from an investment. When we use an advisor, we need to evaluate what we end up with after all is said and done in their pretty office. We need to compare our returns to those of the same market index. Do we buy groceries based on value or the manufacturer's marketing claims? That is the **tough question**.

One famous investor once said that he only looks at what he gets to keep, not what he's told. In short, if we give an advisor $5,000 a year for 20 years, how much will we get back, net, net, after fees, charges, commissions and taxes. If we give them $100,000, how much will we receive in 20 years?

The easiest way to evaluate an advisor's value is to compare our asset value to the market value for the same asset and same timeline. If they invested in stocks, we should expect more than $400,000 back. If we received less than $300,000, we need to question our advisor or shop for another. $100,000 should grow to $1 million. Use this calculator to compare your rate of return: http://www.moneychimp.com/calculator/compound_interest_calculator.htm

Most retail brokers and advisors sell their firm's products. They share commissions and fees as they offer products designed for *firm* revenue. Most products are structured to provide the firm with high revenue and are not the best products for the average investor. Average investors earn only 2.56%. DALBARinc.com

I think the trend to commoditization will continue to degrade the financial advice business. Why should a person of modest means (less than a million dollars) bother to pay costs of 1-3% for the same results as those of the low-cost investor?

The greatest investor of our time thinks **compounding creates wealth**, not specific advisor products or stock picks:

"My wealth has come from a combination of living in America, some lucky genes, and **compound interest.**" *Warren Buffett*

If wealthy people have become wealthy by compounding high-return assets as Buffett says, then more people will realize that wealth comes from **compound interest**, not from brokers or "professional" money managers. It seems that more and more people will learn that all they have to do to be successful is maximize the compounding of their money.

Warren Buffett's cost basis, what he paid for the businesses his company owns, is so low he can make money no matter what happens each quarter, year or even decade. He bought Coke in 1987. However, Coke may not be a good deal now. Buffett holds businesses that sell jewelry, soda, underwear, bricks, rail shipping, DQ and insurance. berkshirehathaway.com/subs/sublinks.html

He advises that the average investor would be better off buying a market index fund (page 24) and letting compounding make them rich. Over time, the stock market earns 10-12%.

The wealthy insist on paying lower fees, charges, commissions and taxes. They buy only what they need so their costs—sales commissions, fees, loads—are less. They don't use our retail brokers and advisors because they know our retail salespeople only use our firms' high-cost products. The wealthy have learned their investment edge is the miracle of compounding, not our star money manager who attracts new "hot" money.

When our star salespeople succeed in attracting assets, we directors can count on larger fee revenue for the coming years. This is what keeps the firm profitable.

No matter how much the wealthy earn, they know it is better to pay fewer taxes so their investments can **compound** faster year over year. Our wealthiest clients have the money to use the best legal services to find ways to pay less in taxes. For instance, Warren Buffett, with $60 billions, pays only 17% **total** tax: http://www.youtube.com/watch?v=Cu5B-2LoC4s. Mitt Romney only **14%**, John Kerry only **13%** and Apple just **9.8%**.

Our clients are using legal means to control the taxes they pay. For instance, a business owner can pay a small salary and pay a lower tax rate on dividends and gains. They can use a variety of corporate and partnership structures, here and in foreign countries to reduce or delay all their taxes.

So we can conclude that another strategy that the wealthy use is low or no taxation. Mr Buffett has said that the delay in recognizing capital gains represents a huge tax-FREE loan from the government. We only pay tax at the time we sell assets—NO SALE, NO TAX. Many like Buffett give their assets away so they will ultimately pay no taxes.

The wealthy know that compounding works best when they put ALL their money to work in successful businesses with few taxes or fees. They don't stop investing if their businesses have a bad day or month or even year. They realize that they can't sustain compounding with a buy and sell trading method. No business person buys a business and then sells it 3 months later like financial advisors do. This activity creates taxes and fees. Bad business for you, not for them!

On the other hand, our retail brokers and advisors may use the fact that Buffett's Coke stock price has dipped to call our retail customers to generate commissions. However, retail customers may end up losing money because the business value may not be there for long. When brokers have another 'good' idea, they tell their customers to sell Coke and buy something else. The transactions help the retail salesperson meet their revenue quota for the month but may not help their clients' long term return.

Wealthy people like Mr Buffett buy millions of dollars of stock like Coke *ONLY* after they understand the company value will not be hurt by a non-critical event, like the crash of 1987. This provided Buffett's buy price with a "**margin of safety**," as his mentor, Benjamin Graham, called it. Buffett waits for this non-critical event and then pounces so his investment can't lose money. And since his holding period is "forever," he does not pay capital gains taxes as it rises. He buys and holds for compound interest.

Another strategy of those who already have wealth is diversification. If one of their businesses slows, they still earn money year over year. They would like to compound as much of their money as possible. Using 'legal' means, they avoid taxes on their accumulations and later on their withdrawals.

Wealthy business owners typically have **only 21%** of their net worth in their own businesses. They own stocks, mutual funds, land, office buildings, and other assets they believe will increase in value. Their debt is usually business debt not personal debt like a mortgage on a large mansion. They are more likely to be your plumber than the TV image of a millionaire.

Diversification is important to any person or institution with long-term investing as a goal. Pension funds like the one for

California state workers (CalPERS) have 63% equities, 23% fixed income and 14% other assets like real estate, forests, etc. Very little is in risky investments like hedge funds or gold.

To avoid investing at the wrong time—at the top of the markets—our clients are constantly buying assets not trading. To avoid missing a market low point, they invest their large cash flow automatically. **Compounding wealth** requires consistency. Those with wealth may hold assets in cash equivalents for a time in anticipation of a large investment opportunity, but they know that being out of the market for very long is dangerous. The market advances in spurts and no one can forecast them in advance.

Warren Buffett's number one rule is "never lose money." To avoid making unwise investment decisions, our clients consider long and hard before trading stocks. They make and follow their investment policy religiously. They consult their attorney and accountant more than a financial advisor.

What does all this mean to you?

My vision of the future is one of simplicity. I think most investors will gravitate to low-cost mutual funds and tax-FREE trusts and no-load discount brokers. They will avoid Wall Street's fees of 1-3% and avoid taxes FOREVER if they can. They will recognize the benefits of the **miracle of compounding**. The steps to let ALL their money compound have been made easier to execute. They will simply set it up themselves and let most of their wealth grow without our assistance and expenses.

It does not take a lot of time to manage an account. Remember, our clients have been building wealth for some time so they already know how their accounts work. It takes only an hour per year to manage most of them. I think simplicity will be the goal for most of them. As master investor Warren Buffett said:

We continue to make more money when *snoring* than when active.
Berkshirehathaway.com

These people have learned that building wealth is more about NOT doing something with their investments. Activity in investing usually is the result of fear or greed. Activity usually costs more than the gains. They only act after considerable discussion with the folks they trust and Wall Street is usually not on their list.

They have learned that building a lifetime business takes patience and time. They have learned to live below their means. They have patiently invested in their own businesses and the businesses owned by the mutual funds they bought long ago.

I think this simplicity trend has already begun. I have noted that during this last recession, the only large mutual fund complex that attracted money was Vanguard Group. Investors are moving from high-cost managed mutual funds to the largest fund provider. With costs under 0.2% compared with our 1-3% expense, people are realizing that "cost matters."

I think they are learning that the number one factor in building wealth is **maximizing the miracle of compounding**. They know that they must allow their money to grow without taxes or fees. They use a number of methods to provide tax-advantaged income all their lives. These methods have meant millions of dollars extra in the accounts. Taxes are the greatest killer of wealth. Fees are easily controlled. Vanguard provides both low-cost index funds AND low-cost managed funds.

Most mutual funds have licensed financial advisors who are salaried, not commissioned. This provides those who need some assurance with less biased confirmation of their own investment choices. So, the younger or up-and-coming millionaires can easily get help when they need it without a formal and costly Wall Street relationship. The larger fund firms can provide most of the services that are provided by our full service Wall Street brokerage firms. Discount brokers have many of the same services for less if the wealthy wish to hold securities at no cost and no taxes until they sell.

My industry has changed and the trend is focused on you, the investor and away from us, the middle people. You may not need your advisor anymore. You may find that you KEEP more by using the less-biased low-cost assistance of the big fund families.

In summary, you can use the time-tested strategies Buffett uses to maximize returns. That's what it's all about even if you continue to use your advisor.

Everything else is hype.

1

How do they help you avoid taxes?

One of the strategies of the wealthy is to avoid taxes on their accumulations. Consider these examples: Buffett **17%**, Romney **14%**, Kerry **13%** and Apple **9.8%**. Most of the top 1% pay far less than the average citizen of this country in terms of disposable income.

If the average family earns $85,000, they pay about 14% federal, 13% SS/Med/UC/Health, 10% state/local, 4% sales/excise, or over 30% total taxes. As Buffett said, "I pay 17.7% total tax. My office staff pays at 32.9%." Of course this does not include pension and other insurance deductions most Americans also pay.

This is why the wealthy avoid taxes with their own businesses and various tax-advantaged vehicles. In order to become and stay wealthy, people need to have money to invest. The average family has no money to build wealth let alone have enough for retirement.

Corporations and businesses can control taxes as an expense by using all the legal means they can afford to pay for. Apple was hauled before Congress in 2013 to explain how it avoids the rate the IRS code mandates—35%. It has subsidiaries around the world so its lawyers and accountants can avoid taxes.

Nearly every major firm has its share of tax tricks up its sleeve. Apple accomplishes this feat with a two-pronged tax strategy. For domestic sales, the company pays profits as a royalty on a subsidiary it owns in Ireland, which are then routed to a tax haven. For overseas sales, the company uses a second Irish sub, routes the profits through The Netherlands to avoid European taxes, and then sends its profits to its tax haven via the first Irish sub. This sub is called a "**disregarded entity**"—an affiliate not subject to U.S. income tax. (This strategy is called the "Double Irish with a Dutch Sandwich," this report says.) Wish we had one.

Some smart working folks have found a way to buyout their boss after working at a skilled trade for years. Some wealthy people have followed this path. They are *The Working Millionaires*. They have learned that building wealth takes time. Most of our wealthy clients own a business or two. It may take a lifetime to make it a sustainable income source and possible retirement treasury. They eventually learn to utilize the system and save on taxes and fees. That is really the only way most Americans can become wealthy.

Some clients have built their wealth by using some of their salary, partnerships or other relationships with others. They invested their money, usually in opportunities that were not open to the public. Others just worked hard and invested. They accumulated $1 million or so over time using a mutual fund or broker.

If you do not have a business to help avoid taxes, one of the best ways for a salaried person to accumulate your first $1 million is to use a tax-FREE account called a Roth IRA. You can avoid all taxes on your investments as they grow and on withdrawals. This account is offered by all the large mutual fund companies like Vanguard, Fidelity, TIAA-CREF, and Schwab.

You can then buy mutual funds or securities that can earn 10% to 12% a year, year after year. You could probably put other investments in this account, but we need to understand the reward and risk characteristics of stocks. I will explain why stocks are the most secure investment for long-term wealth-building below.

For now, you need to consider the fact that if we want to have a balance of $1 million; we would have to wait 100 years for a minimum contribution of say $250 a month to grow in a CD at 2%. Investing in stocks provides almost the reverse risk profile. Historically, the value of a stock market index—a bunch of stocks —has varied greatly in any one year. However, over time, the value has ALWAYS increased. This is the reason wealthy people have most of their money in the stocks of growing companies.

Remember, we are looking for an investment that compounds our money at 10-12% year after year. The reward and risk profile of owning a bunch of stocks is like owning a business —in any one year, we might have a loss or we might profit. But over time we have more profits than losses and thus succeed.

After you are wealthy, you can leave some of your money in CDs and US treasuries for liquidity purposes. Bank savings are a great place to park our money for a year in case you need it to take advantage of an investment opportunity.

However, bank savings are not really an investment. People who put all their money in the bank because they think it is "safe" are not thinking about the long-term. They are actually losing money. Inflation is eating away at the value of their savings.

Inflation is historically about 3%. If we earn 3% or less on our money, we are losing purchasing power. Wealthy people make sure part of their portfolio is liquid. They don't want to have to sell one of their businesses or one of their long-held securities in order to raise cash for any reason. This activity creates taxes.

There are few investments that we can buy that have the same long-term annual returns of stocks of growing companies. The graph below presents the relative growth of different types of investments and inflation.

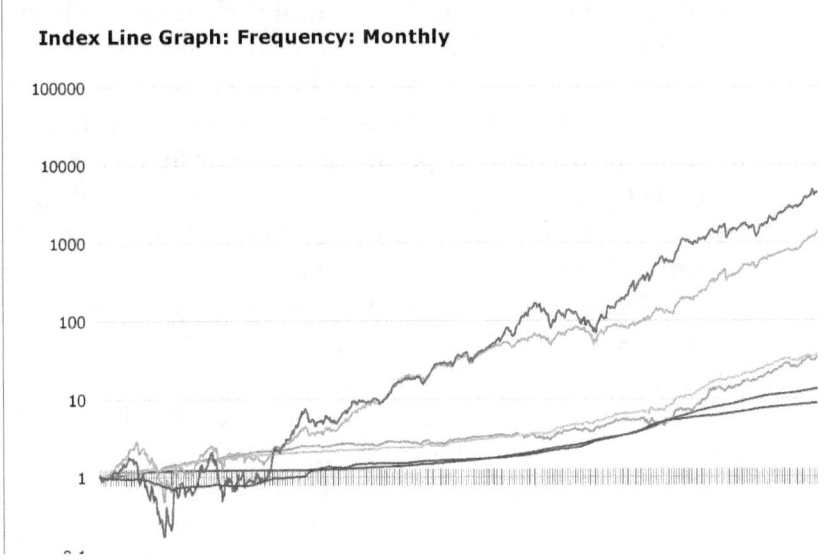

Index Line Graph: Frequency: Monthly

Top line—Small Cap Stocks
2nd line—Large Cap Stocks (S&P 500)
3rd line—US Long-term Corporate Bonds
4th line—Intermediate-term Government Bonds
5th line—US 30 day Government T-bills
6th line—US inflation

Courtesy: Dr. Campbell R. Harvey http://www.duke.edu/~charvey/

Over long-periods of time, government bonds grow at a rate a little above the rate of inflation. Large company stocks like GE and P&G grow at a higher rate and thus accumulate larger values in our account. Smaller companies grow much faster and make our account even larger over time. However, as the graph shows, the index line can be very jagged on a monthly and even yearly basis. Values do go up over time.

This graph makes it pretty clear that in order to accumulate $1,000,000 from monthly contributions, we must buy and hold the securities of growing companies worldwide AND pay **zero** tax on the growth to maximize compounding. We can see clearly that investing in growing company stocks is more likely to get us to our goal in our lifetime than investing in government bonds or a bank savings account.

This graph shows the accumulation over time without paying taxes each year on our earnings or annual fees to an advisor or broker. It does show that over most periods greater than 10 years, our account value grows more with stocks.

Some wealthy people also invest in gold, real estate, and alternative investment schemes. But these investments do NOT usually represent a large portion of their portfolio. These investments do not come without significant costs and significant risk. They do NOT show the same consistent long-term growth pattern that global growing companies do.

As your investments grow—especially mutual funds that pay dividends and gains each year—you will not have to pay tax on them because of your special IRS-approved account. Most regular IRAs and pension accounts are tax-DEFERRED not tax-FREE. Taxes have to be paid sometime.

Your Roth IRA allows you to leverage tax-FREE accumulations over time against an immediate tax deduction as with a regular IRA or 401k pension. The benefits can be enormous. For instance, if you make contributions of $250 a month, $3,000 a year to your low-cost stock mutual funds, you could spend $30,000 tax-FREE for every $3,000 you deposited!

You invest $99,000 and grow your account to $1 million in about 33 years, $2 million in 40 and $3 million in 42. You pay no tax on the reinvested dividends and gains as your account grows and NO tax when you spend your accumulations. And, you can avoid Wall Street's commissions, fees, loads, and charges. Some savvy investors have already decided to go this route. I would be surprised if more didn't follow.

If an investment requires taxes and fees to be paid each year, this cancels some of the compounding effect on the total accumulation over time. Since we wish to reach our first $1 million as soon as possible, we must use a tax-FREE account to hold our investments. Without this account, we may reduce our total accumulation by half because we lose the compounding effect. The chart below gives us an idea of what can happen over time.

Tax-FREE v Taxable

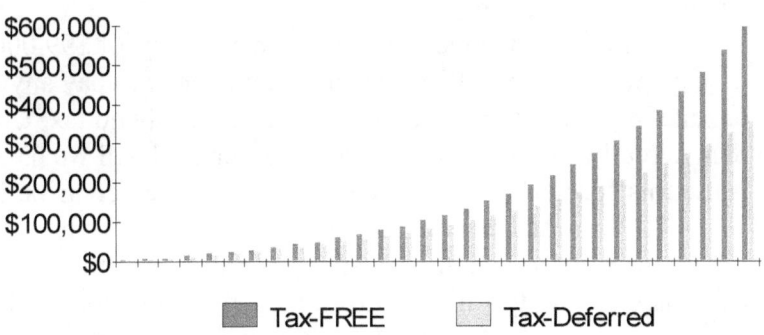

The American tax system taxes earned income at higher rates than investment income. Thus we must pay federal and state income taxes, excise taxes, Social Security and Medicare taxes, perhaps unemployment and disability income taxes as well as sales tax on most goods.

Traditional pensions, 401k and IRAs just delay taxes—taxes must be paid later as the money comes out of the account AND at higher **earned income** tax rates. Thus even when our investment money is growing it is converted to earned income money for tax purposes. Unlike Mr Buffett, we would NEVER get to pay the wealthy people rate of 15% without a tax-FREE trust.

Luckily, there is now a solution for you to match the tax advantage of the wealthy. In fact, only you can use it. Warren Buffett and Mitt Romney earn too much to use this trust.

Senator Roth introduced the Roth IRA in 1997. This tax-FREE account provides the protection you need to allow your contributions to compound without taxation every year AND later when you take them out, you **never have to pay taxes** on the earnings, dividends and interest you earn on your money. You don't even pay the tax-advantaged rate of the wealthy!

Ben Franklin was wrong! Only death is certain, not taxes. The only thing you give up with this account is an immediate tax deduction. This is a better deal than most wealthy people have. Tax-FREE accumulation and tax-FREE income after age 59.5 is a huge bonus. It is like receiving $250,000 FREE on your $1 million account. Also, because you already paid tax on the contributions, you pay no tax when you borrow contributions during your lifetimes. This can make a big impact on your borrowing costs when you take money out to buy an appliance, a car, a down payment or living expenses.

Using this account, our total contributions of $99,000 over time grow to over $1,000,000 and we don't have to pay any federal or state income tax on the earnings. Since we pay no tax, Uncle Sam is really helping us out in meeting our goal. All we have to do is use this special IRS tax haven and keep making contributions.

This special account is the IRS §408 trust. We have to follow the rules to gain this amazing tax advantage but the Roth IRA rules are pretty simple—taxed money goes in and tax-FREE earnings come out after age 59 ½. You can take your contributions out anytime.

Why is this account special? Every other type of investment account requires that taxes be paid now or later. Mutual funds declare gains each year just like a bank CD and we need to pay tax. Our retirement accounts and annuities are tax-deferred. We pay tax when we take money out. Even life insurance with cash value requires taxes to be paid unless it is a death benefit to heirs. Even assets like individual stocks or ETFs or our own company equity held for long term gains will require taxes eventually when sold.

Contributions are limited to $5,500 (2013), but may rise in future years. http://www.irs.gov/publications/p590/ch02.html There are income limits but most people don't hit the earnings limit of $128,000 (2013) until later. If we are married, the limit is $188,000 (2013).

We may also invest in our employer's Roth 401k if it is offered. The contributions grow tax FREE forever. We can contribute up to $17,500 (2013). We will have tax-FREE income from the account later.

We can make contributions to our Roth 401k only if our

employer offers it in the retirement plan. Many young people prefer to be taxed at the beginning of their careers since their salaries do not draw high tax rates yet. The contribution limit may be raised in the future.

There are no limits on an employee's income in determining if he or she can make designated Roth 401(k) contributions. If we decide to invest $10,000 a year for 35 years in a low-cost stock fund inside our employer's Roth 401k plan, we could accumulate $2 million with NO income taxation to pay on the earnings. The tax savings might be worth an extra 30% since our federal and state tax payments are avoided.

The catch: If we take the *earnings* out before age 59.5, we must pay income tax, unless we use $10,000 for our first home, are disabled, or die. The account must be open at least 5 years to take money out. However, if we take out **contributions**, we pay no tax. If we pay our 'loan' back to our own account, we can still reach our goal. The hard part is leaving our money alone to grow tax-FREE.

Let's say we need $20,000 to buy a new used car. As we can see from the chart on page 22, taking $20,000 from an account worth $250,000 is very different from taking $20,000 from one worth only $30,000. Both are contributions and are not taxable but borrowing 60% of the account this early stunts its growth.

The payoff: The chart below shows how your money can grow tax-FREE and fee-FREE. When you and your spouse contribute $250 a month to your Roth IRAs, your family can accumulate enough for retirement and serious medical needs. You might even have enough for an inheritance. This shows the power of compounding without Wall Street. You clean up on Wall Street!

Monthly	Accumulation at 12% per year									
	5	10	15	20	25	30	35	40	45	50
$100	$8,167	$23,004	$49,958	$98,925	$187,884	$349,496	$643,095	$1,176,477	$2,145,469	$3,905,834
$200	$16,334	$46,008	$99,916	$197,850	$375,768	$698,992	$1,286,190	$2,352,954	$4,290,938	$7,811,668
$300	$24,501	$69,012	$149,874	$296,775	$563,652	$1,048,488	$1,929,285	$3,529,431	$6,436,408	$11,717,502
$500	$40,835	$115,020	$249,790	$494,625	$939,420	$1,747,480	$3,215,475	$5,882,385	$10,727,346	$19,529,169

The Roth IRA Rules

Contributions:

$5,500 ($6,500 over age 50) each year
Income under $128,000 (2013) single
married $188,000 (2013)

Distributions:

Tax-FREE for contributions.
And Tax-FREE for earnings if
Over age 591/2,
Account open 5 years,
Taxable earnings unless
Disabled,
First home ($10,000),
Death

Bonus:

Account can grow tax-FREE for life
Minimum distribution rules don't apply
Heirs don't pay income tax
Account has no maximum

Check with your tax preparer
www.IRS.gov/pub/irs-pdf/p590.pdf

2

Did they provide a lifetime investment plan?

Our working millionaire would find a way to save the $20,000 separately or keep driving the old car. The power of compounding is too valuable to lose by raiding the account too early. One story about billionaire Buffett will illustrate the habits of the wealthy. Mr Buffett is said to have driven (no chauffeur) his VW Beetle long after he became a multimillionaire. Buffett did not like to lose money and a new car loses 40% of its value quickly. He thought that the $35,000 a new car cost, invested at 10-12% is worth about $80,000 in 10 years. So he kept driving his old VW.

Most clients are not that thrifty. However, if your income has not yet exceeded the Roth IRA limit, you can use your tax-FREE contributions to buy without paying loan interest. You pay cash for a used car to avoid new car depreciation and new appliances, vacations, and other necessities. AFTER you have let your contributions compound, you can "borrow" them interest FREE. When **both** family wage earners contribute to their Roth IRAs, you can easily reach a quarter of a million dollars in 15 years. That means $90,000 are contributions and then some of them can be used to pay cash instead of buying on credit.

Our clients pay cash because then they never PAY interest. Paying interest on non-income producing assets is the reverse of compounding. Someone else is becoming wealthy from them. The wealthy always EARN interest. They use this calculator moneychimp.com/calculator/compound_interest_calculator.htm to determine what the real cost of buying something on credit will be just as Buffett did. Why give up $80,000 when we can drive the old car a little longer? Buffett could have bought 100 new cars and it wouldn't have changed his wealth or lifestyle, but he didn't. His habit is to live frugally. He still lives in his first $31,500 home.

You can use this account (its contributions) to cover your liability insurance deductibles if needed. Over time, you can save thousands of dollars by using the highest deductibles on your car, home and health insurance. **Self-insurance** is also the way to avoid any changes in your policy costs. Insurers are less likely to drop you if you don't make claims for small amounts. If you take care of your out-of-pocket medical expenses, you may find a low-cost comprehensive policy if you need to buy health coverage.

The rules for the use of your Roth IRA account are manageable by yourself. You don't need an advisor. They are found at irs.gov/retirement/article/0,,id=137307,00.html. Your account trustee can answer most questions. You don't need to pay an attorney. All of the large low-cost mutual funds firms are trustees. I will discuss the best firms available below.

You can start this account with any of the firms with no upfront charges. Most do charge an annual fee for the initial investments. Charges are reduced later. We will consider the specific investment options later. We will use low-cost firms because you will keep more of your own money. You don't need to pay Wall Street to maintain this account.

It is important to pick a trustee with the least costs since over time the annual costs can really destroy your accumulations. For instance, if you use a brokerage firm like ours as trustee, you might have to pay 2-3% or more each year on the balance. The difference is huge. If both spouses have a low-cost account with contributions of $250 a month for 37 years, they could accumulate $3,000,000. If they use a high-cost broker/advisor, both accounts may hit only $1,300,000. Depending on earnings of 8-10% and total costs of 2% per year, you could really hurt yourself. You need to watch the costs. Advisors do NOT beat the markets over the long term. Just stick with your investment plan.

You can open your account at any age as long as you have *earned* income. Stock dividends or interest do not count. I can't use a Roth unfortunately. Any job will do. You don't even need a job requiring a W-2 to prove it. A part-time, weekend or night job will do. Any cash-only work will qualify—even for a child. I think accountants recommend that receipts and records be maintained. You could even work for yourself in a home-office business.

Nontaxable distributions from a Roth IRA won't affect your eligibility for student aid either. Later, in retirement, this money won't affect your social security benefits as of the rules today.

You can make contributions to both your individual Roth IRA and your Roth account at work (401k, 403b, 457b). The limits change each year, so check Pub 590: http://www.irs.gov/pub/irs-pdf/p590.pdf. The 2013 limits are $5,500 ($1,000) and $17,500 ($5,500) respectively. The 2013 limits are $5,500 ($1,000) and $17,500 ($5,500). (We can make a catch-up contribution to both.)

Higher income earners can build a non-deductible IRA and then convert it to a Roth IRA, paying taxes on the converted amount in stages. The higher tax-FREE accumulations later on justify an immediate tax bill for those who do tax planning.

Avoiding taxes on your annual gains supercharges your accumulations. This special account is the IRS §408 trust or Roth IRA. You have to follow the rules of a Roth IRA to gain this amazing tax advantage. The rules are pretty simple: pay smaller taxes on contributions now in exchange for NO tax on huge gains later. You can borrow the contributions to avoid paying interest to banks for our major purchases. You earn interest, you don't pay interest. This is the perfect tax shelter for any working person. And you can beat Wall Street because it is free to set up and run each year. In the future, we can spend tax-FREE $30,000 for every $3,000 we invest today.

See the client account below: $1 million in 32 years. He never let Wall Street touch his money.

It is important to just stick with the investment plan. The *Miracle of Compounding* does the work, not stock pickers.

Actual client Tom's account, investing $3,000 per year, 1962-2003

24%	253, 720
16%	294, 315
12%	329, 633
-10%	296, 670
24%	367, 870
11%	408, 336
-8%	375, 669
4%	390, 696
14%	445, 393
19%	530, 018
-14%	455, 815
-26%	337, 304
37%	462, 106
24%	573, 011
-8%	527, 171
6%	558, 801
18%	659, 385
32%	870, 388
-5%	826, 869
22%	1, 008, 780
21%	185,920
6%	200,255
32%	268,297
19%	322,843
5%	342,135
17%	403,808
32%	536,987
-3%	523,787
31%	690,091
8%	748,538
10%	826,692
2%	846,286
38%	1,172,015
23%	1,445,268
33%	1,926,197
28%	2,469,372
21%	2,991,570
-9%	2,725,059
-12%	2,403,420
-22%	1,874,601
29%	2,412,905

3

What have been other clients' returns over 20 years?

As Reagan said, we need to "trust, but verify" our advisor's promises. There is no other way to know if they are doing a good job. The wealthy get richer just by leaving their money invested. **Compounding high earnings is your *best* strategy.** The rich don't work more hours or take more risks. The famous 1% at the top of society take down 23.5% of all income (up from 8.9% 30 years ago). They don't work any harder than you do—their money does.

Because of compounding, many millionaires have said, "the first million was the hardest." If a working business person has accumulated $250,000, it takes her or him 20 years to grow it to $1,000,000 using tax-advantaged investments. However, it only takes 7-9 years to double their money. Investors in stock funds, earning 10-12% on average, can double it again to $2 million in less than 10 years without adding new money. Their tax-advantaged accounts make it easier to reach their goal. It is compounding that makes it happen—not Wall Street brokers.

Compounding of high earnings means that we make money on our last period's accumulations. The progression looks like the client's account values on the previous page. Notice that our balance can double in a couple of good years. This happens because we are not just adding $3,000 per year, but adding up to 38% of the previous year's accumulation to our balance. We are making money on top of our money with no extra effort on our part. During this 40 year period, this client lost money some years. In fact, they lost 14% and then 26% back to back, but then made 37% and 24%.

Wealthy people don't panic. They have learned that compounding over the long-term is the only way they can build wealth. There are no successful get rich quick schemes. To reach their goal, they know there will be setbacks. No business grows steadily upward all the time. They have seen the losses before and they don't sell their assets in a panic.

We will buy assets that "grow by themselves." We will have security because our ***purchasing power*** will grow over time. If we doubt that the wealthy invest in the stock market for security, take a look at the long-term returns for various Vanguard mutual funds where they put their money. These funds have provided investors with $1,000,000 or more for their retirement. During the recent recessions, Vanguard had inflows not outflows.

The wealthy earn 10% to 12% on their money. Some buy all ten Vanguard funds and receive 11% total return with less risk than owning just one fund. When one fund is down, others are up.

2012 Total Return	Fund	Long-term Return	Longevity
15.8%	500 Index	10.5%*	since 1976
2.7%	Energy	12.3%	since 1984
18.3%	Extended Market	10.3%	since 1987
15.1%	Health	16.3%	since 1984
20.0%	International Growth	10.8%	since 1981
15.3%	PRIMECAP	12.9%	since 1984
18.0%	Small Cap Index	10.4%	since 1960
10.1%	Wellesley Income	10.2%	since 1970
20.8%	Windsor	11.2%	since 1958
16.7%	Windsor II	10.4%	since 1985
15.3%	Average	11.5%	

*Average Annual Returns as of 12/31/12.

This kind of security comes from our regular contributions … and patience. The miracle of compounding works its magic on our Roth IRA account when we give it TIME. The wealthy give their money time to compound. They don't take it out and they try not to pay tax every year on the gains. They maintain their contribution schedule because each $100 added is worth $10,000 to them later. They use the compound interest calculator so they know the future value: moneychimp.com/calculator/compound_interest_calculator.htm.

Compounding of high earnings requires patience but has a big bang. Most people who become wealthy have to wait for years of slow growth in their account. At the beginning of the accumulation, especially if we have a loss or two, we are very tempted to get discouraged and quit making contributions. The account just doesn't seem to adding up to an inspiring total.

It took client Tom 21 years to get to $150,000. Then it only took 14 years to get to a $1,172,015. After only 4 years, it became $3,000,000. Shortly thereafter he "lost" over a million dollars!

This client stuck with it and was successful in reaching the goal but there are many who do not. Most people who are not wealthy already, have a hard time believing it can happen with their patience. They just don't have the experience of how compounding works to keep faith in its outcome eventually.

If you already have an Roth IRA account with significant values, you can use it to do your gift and estate planning. You don't have to take the money out beginning at age 70½, unlike the regular IRA or pension. You can let it grow. You can name your family members as beneficiaries which will be effective for both property law and income tax purposes. Obviously, as beneficiary, your grandchild could just liquidate the account and thus lose the value for their "Gift of a Lifetime." Wealthy people use a knowledgable attorney to make sure their wealth passes to those who make the most of it.

Once an account becomes sizable, we don't need to add contributions to it. Usually, by the time we stop regular employment, we aren't making contributions. This account cannot accept contributions unless they are the result of earned income. Some wealthy people continue to work after age 65 because they love what they do and want to continue. Obviously, they don't need to work. The **miracle of compounding** continues to work.

One of the best examples of the potential of growth by compounding is seen in the accumulation of investor Anne Scheiber. With below average wages, this woman invested in quality companies which paid dividends and gains. She reinvested her dividends and gains and at her death gave $22 million to Yeshiva University for a scholarship designed to help support deserving women.

The Miracle of Compounding doubles our money in 7-9 years when we put it to work in high earning company stocks. We don't have to do anything except let it work. Warren Buffett reminds us that this is the key to investing success.

The annual returns of growing companies

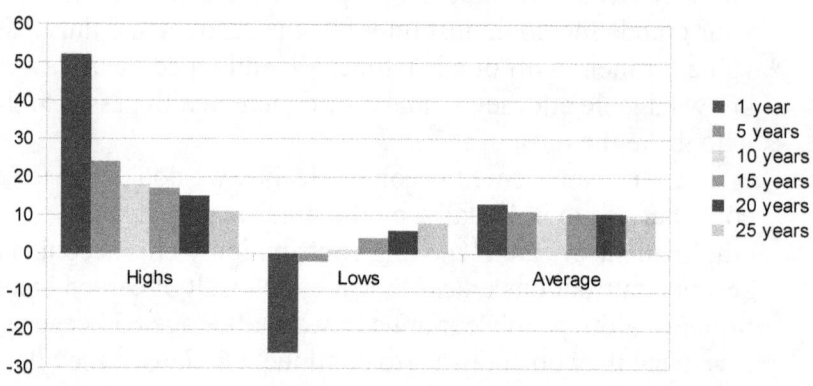

Range of annual returns of stocks, 1950 – 2000

4

Is their investment plan consistent?

To grow wealth, we have to maintain consistent contributions to it. It seems self evident but I guess if we don't learn to put money away early in our lives, there is always an emergency for our cash.

When we develop the habit of investing, we take our emotions out of the process. If we do not watch the stock market or our account balance regularly, we will be less likely to panic. If we don't have to write and send the contribution each month, we don't think about how our account is doing.

Most people want to watch their money. They have no experience of building a business by putting their own money into it and sometimes seeing the VALUE go down. But the business does not fail. It continues. We, as a silent partner must learn to live with this rise and fall. We have to believe that not all global businesses will fail. They will continue to grow. We need to think of this account as our stake in growing businesses.

One way we can help change our thinking is to put the account out of our immediate concern by making the contributions automatic. Like the Social Security contributions we make every payday, the contributions come out of our pay automatically. This can happen easily with a Roth 401k since our Plan administrator will deduct the amount we specify at Plan enrollment. In the same manner, we can have the Roth IRA trustee debit our checking account automatically every period.

As one client told me, "I never see the deduction, so I never miss it." Of course this client has already identified the $250 he has committed to his $1,000,000 future. He says that he would just waste the $250 anyway. He had been doing that for years because he never took the trouble to set his goals for short-term and long-term timelines. He took my advice and went through his spending on financial services. He used our Guides to find the $250 a month he was wasting on products and services he would never use or need. In Dan Keppel's amazon.com/Insiders-Guides-Discount-

Financial-Services/ you will find **"tricks of the trade"** that we insiders use to buy directly from quality manufacturers.

Many people have trouble keeping up the habit of investing every month. Some emergency always interupts this process. The delay in the periodic contributions causes the compounding effect to be reduced. The interruption is like starting the investment process late. This chart shows us what starting early or not putting off the investments can do. Over time, the delay compounds the lack of accumulation. Starting 5 years later means ending up with HALF the amount we were shooting for. It is hard to believe that missing that $250 a month for 5 years or $15,000 can reduce our total from $600,000 to $300,000. It's easy to say **I will start later**.

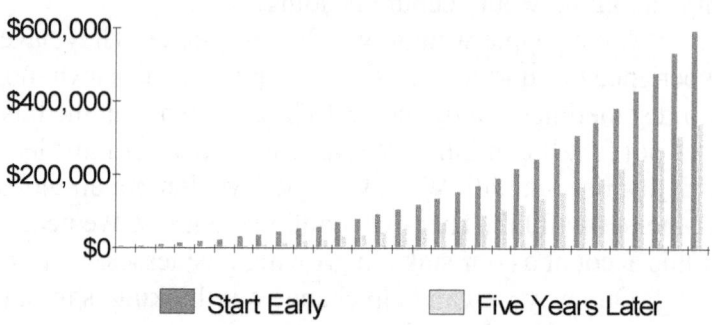

This is why our contributions to the account should not pass through our hands. We should have the money taken directly from our bank account by the trustee. Contributions are after-tax so you can take them back, if necessary, with no tax payable. Nontaxable distributions from a Roth IRA won't affect your eligibility for student aid either. Later, in retirement, this money won't affect your Social Security benefits as of the rules today.

The second reason why this technique for developing wealth works is that when contributions are automatic, we do not have the temptation to try to time the market. Many people want to know the secret to timing the market so that they can invest right at the bottom of market cycles and sell at the peak of the market.

Unfortunately, it is a myth that we can do this over time. Again, this is our misconception of how building wealth works.

Yes there are Wall Street gurus who have records. However, they are the exception and we don't know which to pick NOW. We are trying to build wealth over time. We want to end up with $1,000,000 tax-FREE. We are silent partners in building businesses that produce dividends and gains over time. We are not placing our contributions on red or black at the casino.

Our account grows with steady contributions because in the month we buy $250 of company stocks in a mutual fund, we receive less shares when the price is high and more shares when the price is low. Studies have shown that this is better than investing our $3,000 all at once. It is not possible to know when the shares we buy will be at their lowest cost in the year going forward. Again, over time, we will own more shares at the least cost because we are buying more when the price is low.

This can be illustrated by considering how hard it is to find the lowest price at any given time in the market. There were ONLY 40 days from 1950 to 2007 that produced 70% of all the S&P 500 index's total returns. That is 40 out of 14,528. We can't possibly know when to buy into the businesses represented in the mutual fund we are using. We will lose money if we try to become traders who time the market. John Bogle's analysis in *Don't Count on It*, p 169 is correct. I have looked into it.

The key to building wealth is steady growth. We have seen that over time, stocks of growing companies have the most consistent record of providing 10-12% annual returns. We just don't know **which** companies and **which** time to invest are best. Luckily, we don't have to know. We need to understand the bigger picture.

The bigger picture is that we want our account accumulation to grow exponentially. We want to take advantage of the miracle of compounding. Since we don't have a million dollars, we are going to have to be patient to acquire it. We want every dollar we invest to count. We have $250 a month to invest so we have to rely on consistent buying of shares to reach our goal.

Accumulations double in value every 7-9 years if they are concentrated in the top two lines below. Of course the stock market doesn't move up at 10-12% EACH year. However, our wealth account will double and double and double so that by age 65, we could have over $1 million. Notice how the account values in the chart on page 22 for our client Tom move from $1 million to $2 million in 8 years, even with 3 years of losses. Of course, a million dollars will be worth less in the future because of inflation. But we will certainly appreciate our account values later no matter what our contributions are now. Consistency builds wealth.

Cumulative Wealth

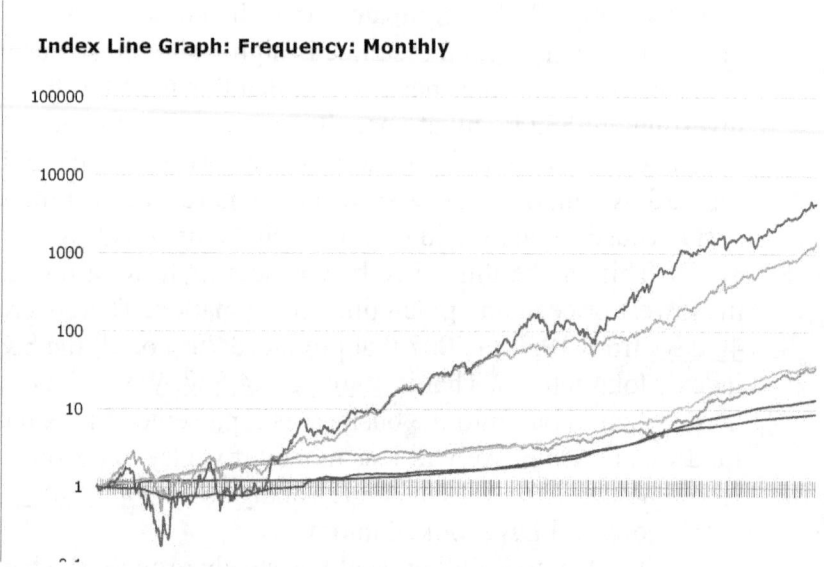

Top line—Small Cap Stocks
2nd line—Large Cap Stocks (S&P 500)
3rd line—US Long-term Corporate Bonds
4th line—Intermediate-term Government Bonds
5th line—US 30 day Government T-bills
6th line—US inflation

Courtesy: Dr. Campbell R. Harvey http://www.duke.edu/~charvey/

And the bonus of this geometric account growth is that it does not quit even after we stop adding our monthly contributions. Once the account has reached a certain mass, let's say after 20 years of contributions or $60,000, it will keep compounding. On page 32 we show you how this worked for contributions of $2,000 to a virtual account invested in the U.S. stock market (500 Index) over time.

We can see, in the chart "Cumulative Wealth" above, that over time wealth accumulates at different rates depending on the type of assets we buy. For anyone who invested in smaller companies over any given 15 year period, the benefits were outstanding. For each $1,000 invested in 1940, $3,000,000 was the total return by the 1990's. Investing more cautiously in the large companies of the S&P 500, for instance, our single $1,000 would have grown to almost a $1,000,00 by 2000. Yes, the lines are not perfectly straight, but growing $250 a month to $1 million is definitely worth the ups and downs. Inflation is designated by the bottom line here. Putting all our money in "safe" investments would accumulate at a rate represented by a line near that bottom line.

Of course, these different rates of wealth accumulation assume two important factors—NO taxes and NO costs. We have eliminated the first killer of wealth—TAXES—by using a tax-FREE trust account. Costs of the investment type we use can also kill your total accumulations. My whole industry is built on the extraction of these costs from the accounts of investors like you. You must use low-cost stock funds to obtain high returns.

The main reason people hire Wall Street firms is to "watch" their money. Our clients are paying us millions of dollars for peace of mind. They think that we can see the future and stop any loss in their accounts. Unfortunately, this is just an illusion we maintain.

You can avoid paying us up to 40% of your eventual total wealth by learning to stick with the program. You can just put your contributions on automatic. Your trustee will debit your checking account every month. You can call them when the market scares you. You have a higher probability of meeting your goals over time by not watching. After going through a couple of crises, we forget we are investing in our future and thus we actually create one.

The Miracle of Compounding only happens with consistent contributions. Warren Buffett has never been a stock "trader." He buys and ***holds*** businesses "forever."

Year	Returns	Balance	Balance	Balance	Balance
		$2,000			
1950	31%	$2,620			
1951	24%	$5,729			
1952	18%	$9,120			
1953	-1%	$11,009			
1954	52%	$19,773			
1955	31%	$28,523			
1956	5%	$32,049			
1957	-11%	$30,304			
1958	43%	$46,194			
1959	12%	$53,978			
1960	1%	$56,538			
1961	26%	$73,757			
1962	-8%	$69,697			
1963	24%	$88,904			
1964	16%	$105,449			
1965	12%	$120,342			
1966	-10%	$110,108			
1967	24%	$139,014			
1968	11%	$156,526			
1969	-8%	$145,844	2,000		
1970	4%	$153,757	2,080		
1971	14%	$177,563	4,651		
1972	19%	$213,681	7,915		
1973	-14%	$185,485	8,527		
1974	-26%	$138,739	7,790		
1975	37%	$192,813	13,412		
1976	24%	$241,568	19,111		
1977	-8%	$224,082	19,422		
1978	6%	$239,647	22,707		
1979	18%	$285,144	29,155	2,000	
1980	32%	$379,030	41,124	2,640	
1981	-5%	$361,978	40,968	4,408	
1982	22%	$444,053	52,421	7,818	
1983	21%	$539,724	65,850	11,879	
1984	6%	$574,228	71,921	14,712	
1985	32%	$760,621	97,575	22,060	
1986	19%	$907,519	118,494	28,632	
1987	5%	$954,995	126,519	32,163	
1988	17%	$1,119,684	150,367	39,971	
1989	32%	$1,480,623	201,125	55,402	2,000
1990	-3%	$1,438,144	197,031	55,680	1,940
1991	31%	$1,886,589	260,731	75,560	5,161
1992	8%	$2,039,676	283,749	83,765	7,734
1993	10%	$2,245,843	314,324	94,342	10,708
1994	2%	$2,292,800	322,651	98,268	12,962
1995	38%	$3,166,824	448,018	138,370	20,647
1996	23%	$3,897,654	553,522	172,656	27,856
1997	33%	$5,186,540	738,844	232,292	39,709
1998	28%	$6,641,331	948,281	299,894	53,387
1999	21%	$8,038,430	1,149,839	365,291	67,019
2000	-9%	$7,316,791	1,048,174	334,235	62,807
2001	-12%	$6,447,855	925,203	296,223	57,095
2002	-22%	$5,024,437	722,291	232,316	46,035
2003	29%	$6,459,474	930,787	301,119	61,730
2004	11%	$7,164,483	1,034,274	336,099	70,664
2005	5%	$7,512,677	1,084,540	352,433	74,098
2006	15%	$8,694,884	1,259,259	412,409	90,450
2007	5%	$9,163,538	1,327,133	434,638	95,325
2008	-39%	$5,601,431	813,388	268,074	60,754
2009	27%	$7,116,358	952,155	342,993	79,699
2010	15%	$8,186,112	1,097,278	396,742	93,954
2011	2%	$8,347,378	1,118,894	404,558	95,805
2012	16%	$9,666,264	1,295,679	468,478	110,942
Avg.	12%	12%	11%	13%	10%

Ibbotson Associates **Stocks average 11.4% per year, bonds 5%, CDs 3%.** Stocks have gone up as much as 54% and as low as –43% in 1 year, up to 28% or down to –12% in 5 years, up 20% or down 0% in 10 years, up 18% or up 3% in 20 years. Short term bonds have gone up 14% or up 0% in 1 year, up 11% or up 0% in 5 years, up 9% or up 0% in 10 years, up 10% or up 1% in 20 years. Check market returns for any period you like:

http://www.moneychimp.com/features/market_cagr.htm

5

Do they offer high-cost products?

**"In every single time period and data point tested,
low-cost funds beat high-cost funds."**

According to an unbiased Morningstar study, low-cost mutual
funds beat high-cost funds PERIOD. However, the myth of Wall
Street is that you must pay more for good performance. Not true.
We all know that in most groceries' prices, paying more (for
packaging and TV commercials) does not guarantee the best
product.

Warren Buffett's mentor, Benjamin Graham, advised: "buy
financial products like we buy "groceries, ... not perfume."

The best predictor of your investing and wealth-building
success is **low cost**. It is common sense that there are just too many
variables in the success of growing companies' stocks for anyone
to be able to pick them in advance on a *consistent* basis. A low-cost
stock mutual fund provides the best chance of **maximizing** our
accumulations as the market leaders change over time.

Contrary to Wall Street's hype, it does not matter which
stocks are rising or falling at any given time. If our account holds a
broad representation of stocks and our investment costs are low,
we will benefit over the long haul. We own them all!

This is the smart strategy. When we subtract the costs of
buying and maintaining investments, we give up a lot of the gains.
We can use an online compounding calculator to become familiar
with total accumulations at different rates of return—3, 5, 7, 9, 11:
moneychimp.com/calculator/compound_interest_calculator.htm

Since the annual returns of stock funds have averaged 10-
12% over time, we want to pick the lowest cost mutual fund
available. A stock fund that reflects the overall market is called an
index fund. This kind of fund costs only 0.05% ($5 per $10,000).
Our account will compound at or near the 10-12% over time since

the costs are low compared to ones that charge 1.5-3%. If we use the high-cost stock funds in our account, we will earn 7-8.5% over time. These funds pay managers high salaries with expensive bonuses. The fund owners and sales staff are paid well also. This is the cash cow of Wall Street. You pay for them.

The chart below makes it clear. Over time, the costs we pay each year will cut our total accumulation by a THIRD or more. Instead of compounding at 10-12% annually on average, some people give up 1.5-3% of the earnings on their money to the middle person. They end up with less.

Cost Matters: 0.19% v 1.68%

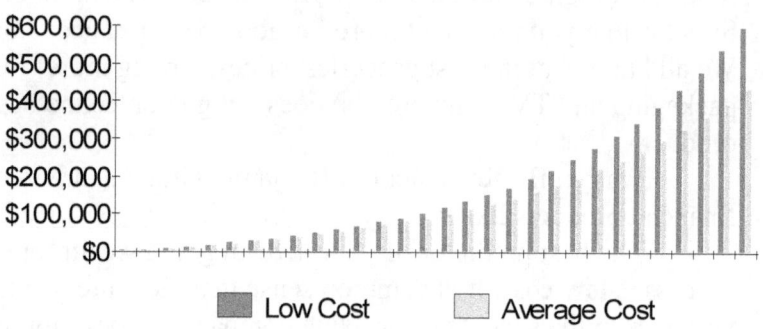

Wall Street says that we can earn more by paying a star manager to pick the right stocks on an ongoing basis. The money "experts" say we get what we pay for and a proven stock-picking manager will overcome the extra costs and make more for us.

The problem is that this myth has been proven wrong. The lowest cost funds don't pay a star manager and owner big bucks but come out ahead over time. There are simply too many variables for anyone or computer program to pick the winning stocks all the time. Some of the lowest cost funds are called index funds. When we buy an index, we are buying a piece of many companies that reflect the market. This gives us the same annual returns as the overall market over time. We pay tiny expenses.

Many studies have proven that index funds beat funds run by stock pickers most of the time. Low-cost index funds beat 86% of funds with a stock-picking manager. *BusinessWeek* Apr 2009. http://www.businessweek.com/investing/insights/blog/archives/200

9/04/where_have_all.html.

When we investigate the experiences of the best money managers and advisors in the world, we find they recommend index funds to most people who invest as silent partners. Here are their statements:

Warren Buffett is probably history's greatest investor, in terms of results with $60 BILLION ($60 thousand million dollars) so far. He buys **companies** that provide valuable services to a great number of people. His company owns parts of Coke, GEICO, Fruit of the Loom, Benjamin Moore, Heinz, Burlington Northern, etc. berkshirehathaway.com/

He told Reuters: "A very low-cost index is going to beat a majority of the amateur-managed money or professionally-managed money."

Compare the odds of selecting the correct mutual fund. A fund's chance of beating the market in EACH year is 3 out of 100. nytimes.com/2009/02/22/your-money/stocks-and-bonds/22stra.html

Peter Lynch, brilliant manager, Magellan Fund "…you'd be just as well off if you'd invested in the S&P 500." *One Up on Wall Street*, 1989, p. 240.

Jonathan Clements, formerly *The Wall Street Journal*
"Most people can do it themselves. ... By indexing, you don't just ensure that you will do better than most other investors. You will also enjoy the advantage of 'relative certainty.' . . . For most investors, Vanguard will be the place to go." *You've Lost It, Now What? How to beat the bear market and still retire on time*, 2003, p. 62, 70.

Charles D. Ellis, money managers' consultant
"The premise . . . that professional investment managers **can** beat the market . . . appears to be false. It is a loser's game. ... clients would have done better in a market fund." Returns are "splendidly predictable—on average and over time." *Investment Policy, How to Win the Loser's Game*, 1985, p. 5, 20, 34.

Jane Bryant Quinn, consumer advisor
"I'm a longtime booster of index mutual funds. These funds follow the market as a whole. Tons of research has shown that most money managers don't beat the markets they invest in, after costs. Maybe your own stocks or funds have excelled in the past couple of years. But in most cases, you've also been taking extra risk. The odds of superior performance are against you, in the long run. Indexing puts the odds on your side." *Los Angeles Business Journal*, May 8, 2000

Charles Schwab founder, discount broker
"I put my money where my mouth is: most of the mutual fund investments I have are in index funds, approximately 75%. My core investments are index funds. Experienced investors have discovered that in any given year, on average, only 20 to 30 percent of mutual funds outperform the market. That is why I recommend index funds…"
Mr. Schwab tells of one of his friends who owned many well-run funds. After keeping track of all the dividends, taxes, reinvestments tax basis and statements, he found he earned the same return as the index of these funds. After selling them all, he bought the index fund. He has "what he wanted in the first place: diversification, tax advantages, one statement, and lower expenses." *Guide to Financial Independence*, 1998, pp. 90, 103, 111.

Motley Fool, Internet site about investing
"Almost *everything* that you will ever read about mutual funds beyond, "Buy an index fund." is superfluous to your long-term success in investing in mutual funds." Fool.com.

Walter Updegrave, senior editor, *Money*
"Mutual fund picking would be easier if there was one you could count on to outperform 70% or so of its competitors over long stretches of a decade or more. It's called an index fund. Although less than 10% of investors own an index fund, they are "one of the best-kept secrets" on Wall Street. My unabashed aim is to convince you to put at least a part of your money into one or more of these funds. You have a far less than a 50% chance of beating the market…. I strongly recommend that you make index funds your primary holding…." *The Right Way to Invest in Mutual Funds*,

1996, p 189-194.

Andrew Tobias, financial writer
"Scrimp and save, putting whatever you can into no-load, low-expense stock market index funds, both U.S. and foreign. You will do better than 80% of your friends and neighbors." *My Vast Fortune*, 1997, p. 158.

There are many books written on the subject of index and "managed" funds. If you wish to vanquish the hype and understand investing, skim *A Random Walk Down Wall Street* by Princeton University's Burton Malkiel. Here are the reasons why smart insiders use low-cost funds:

1. Both stock and bond index funds provide better returns than 86% of managed funds for periods greater than 10 years.
2. You earn more because you pay lower costs and taxes.
3. Low-cost funds build greater wealth over time.
4. Low-cost funds can be less volatile because they reflect whole sectors of the market.
5. Low-cost funds offer better diversification.
6. You know what you are paying for. No high-salary managers.
7. Low-cost funds don't require you to hope the manager will predict the future correctly. The odds of doing it are 1 in 15,000 each year separately. Over time, all funds provide average returns minus their costs.
8. Low-cost funds are easy to buy.

> "Professional money management is a gigantic rip-off."
> Bill Gross, star bond manager, *Everything You've Heard About Investing is Wrong*

Summary of many studies about investing

First, fund managers try to predict the future of the market when they buy and sell securities in their funds. There is no proof this can be done well over time. Yesterday's winners are usually tomorrow's losers. The AVERAGE market return has been 10-12%, so a few managers will beat the average by luck—Just not

the same ones every year. nytimes.com/2008/07/13/business/13stra.html
Second, the costs of the manager, their staff and operations must be paid for by you whether or not they earn you a dime. It is always better to pay as little as possible for the same performance. Costs can take 40% of your returns over time. Surprisingly, while the stock index rose 10%, investors with high paid managers averaged only **2.56%*** annually from 1990-2010 (QAIB). DALBARinc.com.

Third, high cost managers get paid for increasing the size of their funds, not for making you rich. Bringing in more money is a full-time job. It is expensive to market the funds given that there are now thousands available. It is inevitable that popular funds will grow until they produce average returns with high expenses. Managers want to be rich, not right. online.wsj.com/article/ SB10001424127887324059704578471154109438438.html

Fourth, there is much less chance of you being treated poorly by fund management if the structure and governance are customer-oriented like Vanguard's and TIAA-CREF's are.

Fifth, many professional managers and Wall Street insiders place their core assets in low-cost index funds.
http://home.business.utah.edu/finmll/fin6350/individualinvestor_notes.pdf

The best predictor of the success of a mutual fund is its **cost**. Usually the least expensive funds that match market averages beat the more expensive managed funds. Low-cost market index funds buy all the securities represented in a broad market. The goal of an index fund is to match its market. Low-cost index funds have provided returns that beat 80-90% of managed funds over the long-term. No Wall Street guru has been able to predict the future so the returns regress to the mean. The smart money is on the averages not the long shot. We **maximize** the Miracle of Compounding by buying and holding low-cost investments.

"In every single time period and data point tested, low-cost funds beat high-cost funds."

6

Will their investments grow in any economy?

If we want to have a $1,000,000 tax-FREE account, we need a way to make it happen—a strategy. We need to know how and where to invest, invest regularly, invest properly, monitor accumulations along the way, and get help when we need it. We need a clear plan that takes only one hour to set up and only one hour per year to manage. Complicated plans just don't work for most people. Complicated strategies cost more to execute.

Picking *individual* stocks as a strategy is not likely to work for us. Professional managers and day traders have had limited success over time. Our strategy is to build wealth as a silent partner in growing global companies. Since it is unlikely that we (or anyone else) will be able to pick the next 'Google' or 'Apple', we invest in a large group of firms. We do not need to fear picking the wrong one or picking one at the wrong time. As the founder of the largest mutual fund firm, John Bogle, says: "Don't look for the needle. Buy the haystack." This is a proven successful strategy.

Of course, this is contrary to the myth of Wall Street 'professional' gurus. We make our living claiming to find the needles every month and you pay us dearly year after year. We promise that the magical stock pickers can find the next big one and you pay us well because you want to be rich.

Like the lottery, we kid ourselves into thinking that "someone has to win, why not me." We don't believe we are wasting our money even though our rational mind knows that our chance of winning is very low. Managed funds don't beat the market most of the time. The odds are like those of a lottery—18 million to 1. Like the lottery, when we invest in a managed fund to "beat the market" we don't count up the costs of the "tickets." We may buy $25 worth of tickets a week and end up winning $1,000 in a year. We spent $1,200 for $1,000.

In the same manner, a mutual fund manager advertises that their fund has "beaten" the market and so we pay 1.5-3% of our assets every year. Over time we find that while the stock market index rose 10.38% from 1990-2010, we earned only **2.56%** annually. This is what happened to retail investors according to Dalbar's QAIB recent study. DALBARinc.com

Many retail investors keep switching to the hot funds or stocks according to the advertising we run regularly. Some are always chasing the last most successful story. Some buy at the high point because they want the winner. They sell when it falls and they want the next high flier. Over time they never earn the return promised by our managers.

In this way, costs can take 40% of their returns over time. Each time they sell and buy, they give up earnings and perhaps part of their money if they use a sales person charging 5%. Even if they stay with one managed mutual fund that has annual fees of 1.5-3%, they are killing the miracle of compounding.

Using the compounding calculator, we can see that our accumulation drops to $0.6 million if we earn 9% instead of 11% annually. We could have $2 million in 40 years at 11%. moneychimp.com/calculator/compound_interest_calculator.htm

Another Wall Street myth is that investing in market index funds will produce average (mediocre) returns. It is true that the returns will be close to the returns of the market. However, historically the market returns are the ones that are somewhat predictable and not bad. Investing in growing companies provides no guaranteed return but the average returns have held steady since the 1930s when they started keeping records.

Wall Street history is littered with strategies that were said to beat the market. The brilliant stock pickers have also come and gone. Today, though, which one of the new ones are you going to invest with? No one knows. The ONLY thing we really know is that the averages of broad market indexes have produced 10-12% on average over time.

For example, some of our clients use these Vanguard mutual funds which have earned over 11% for a long time. Of course, there is no guarantee of future returns, but they have all done fairly well. Most started with the 500 Index and added companies in the Energy, Health and International sectors. These 10 funds have done well over time. Many investors pick Vanguard funds because the funds are well run **at cost**. No "bells and whistles." No expensive managers and overhead. No owner taking profits from the investment returns.

2011 Total Return	Fund	Long-term Return*	Longevity
1.97%	500 Index	10.36%	since 1976
-1.74%	Energy	12.71%	since 1984
-3.73%	Extended Market	9.96%	since 1987
11.45%	Health	16.30%	since 1984
-13.68%	International Growth	10.50%	since 1981
-1.84%	PRIMECAP	12.79%	since 1984
-2.80%	Small Cap Index	10.26%	since 1960
9.63%	Wellesley Income	10.16%	since 1970
-4.00%	Windsor	11.00%	since 1958
2.70%	Windsor II	10.18%	since 1985
0.00%	Average	11.42%	

*Average Annual Returns as of 12/31/11.

These investors are long-term investors, not speculators. They believe that investments in low-cost funds (index and managed) are their best chance of reaching their goals. They have been rewarded for that belief. Vanguard has many low-cost funds and their service is better than most funds. I own some of them.

Remember, we are investing for the long-term. Most pension funds are invested in stock and bond indexes. Even though the market fell 22% in 2002 and jumped 29% in 2003, the average was still holding. Average returns mean we do not suffer the lowest lows nor the highest highs. They regress to the mean: 10-12%.

Most of the largest growing companies in the world are held by these funds. Large US firms are now earning at least half of their profits overseas so we are benefiting from growth around the world. This is important because we don't want to miss important earnings progress as the developing nations like China and India expand their economies.

We don't know exactly which companies will be winners but we want to participate in all of them. We want to own some smaller growing companies too. If they become successful, they will move to the large company funds. We are exposed to almost all areas of the global economy by buying shares of these mutual funds at the lowest cost. We suffer the ups and downs of the markets just like every investor. However, we see that some funds do better at certain times while others do worse. Together we see clients hitting their goal of 10-12% average annual returns.

This type of investing has the greatest chance of avoiding severe swings in the balance of our accumulation. This type of strategy—investing in different types and sizes of companies in different sectors around the world—is called Modern Portfolio Theory.

Modern Portfolio Theory

Some clients use the MPT strategy to control risk while increasing returns. MPT (Moneychimp.com/articles/risk/riskintro.htm) holds that if we put our eggs in different baskets of assets that grow at different times, then the value of all our eggs grows with fewer ups and downs. We can manage the ups and downs of equity funds by buying different ones over time. Higher risk assets are small caps, REITs and foreign stocks. This strategy earns 10-12% with 30% less volatility.

Members assemble asset classes (see callan.com/research/download/?file=periodic/free/457.pdf) that fit their risk-reward tastes. According to this Nobel Prize-winning strategy moneychimp.com/articles/risk/portfolio.htm, a high return asset with a low correlation to other assets in the portfolio can actually reduce the volatility of the whole. It may be possible to earn high returns with less risk **overall** as each asset goes up and down at different times. See the example at fool.com/personal-finance/retirement/2007/03/06/5-steps-to-salvage-your-retirement.aspx.

The past provides only PROBABLE futures. But isn't $1,000,000 (plus or minus $100,000) better than $150,000. Your $250-per-month deposit in the bank for 33 years will be worth about $100,000 after tax compared with about $1 million from stock investing with no tax. Every investor would be better off with $1 million (+/- $100,000) than $150,000 from a bank.

When young investors begin investing, they cannot buy all 10 Vanguard funds at once with $250 per month. Vanguard has minimums on all funds so they can keep their expenses low for everyone.

There are two ways to start our Roth IRA account. The easiest way is to save $250 a month in our savings account until we have the $1,000 minimum for Vanguard's entry fund: STAR #56. We can open the Roth IRA by phone or online: STAR minimum is $1,000. Most Vanguard funds need $3,000 to start. We can keep contributing to this index fund until we have $3,000 for the 500 Index and then $3,000 for the Extended Market funds. Vanguard is at 800.551.8631.

The second way to begin is to open a Roth IRA at TIAA-CREF, the world's largest pension company, primarily for educational and research institutions. Low expenses and low initial contributions make TIAA-CREF an organization we can stay with for life. TIAA-CREF 800.842.2888.

At TIAA-CREF.org, we can make application and begin immediately with an automatic monthly contribution of $100 or more from our bank account. We can follow how the assets grow by themselves. TIAA-CREF has two funds that provide us with the diversity of companies worldwide: TIAA-CREF Equity Index and TIAA International Equity.

Request a prospectus (owner's manual) for each fund you will be using at Vanguard or TIAA-CREF. Both mutual fund firms have experienced salaried representatives that provide accurate information about accounts and funds. Both offer low-cost index funds that hold a broad representation of the market returns of 10-12%. This is a building block to accumulating wealth.

Both firms are focused on you, not on profits.

This strategy is to buy stocks of growing companies worldwide. No Wall Street guru can predict the future winners. Most can't do better than 50%—a flip of the coin. Your investments provide long-term growth of 10-12% annually on average with the benefit of avoiding single company or industry failures. It provides exposure to new growth potential around the world with less risk than holding one company, one sector, or one country. Some years our account is up 33% and some years down 22%. However, we double our money every 7-9 years *over time.*

It is the amount we KEEP that matters!

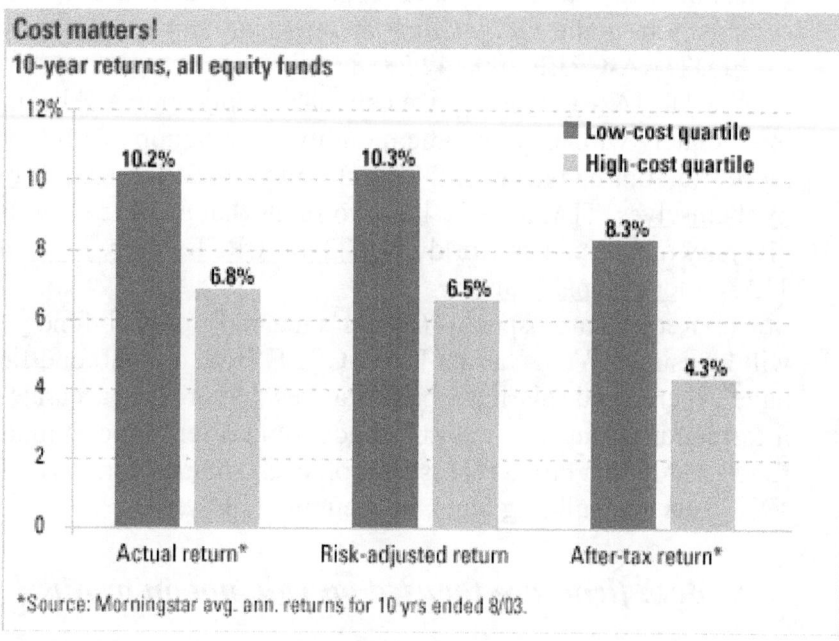

Cost matters!

10-year returns, all equity funds

*Source: Morningstar avg. ann. returns for 10 yrs ended 8/03.

7

Do they provide a Spending Plan?

We need to find at least $250 per month to invest in order to build our account. We can build wealth by following the strategy outlined in the previous chapters, but we need to have at least $250 available in the first place. In my experience, it doesn't matter how much people earn, most say they don't have the money to invest for their future. "Today is hard enough," they complain.

Yes, that may well be, but if we don't find the $250 we won't have a very happy tomorrow. We have to go back to our goal. We want to build wealth: accumulating $1,000,000 over time. Based on the way wealth compounds, we need to identify at least $250 a month on a permanent basis. We need to be consistent for the **miracle of compounding** to work.

Budget is a dirty word so we won't use it. No one wants to be restricted in their spending. Even the people who know they are wasting $100 a month on the lottery, still play. I know it satisfies an immediate riches fantasy. However, people change when they see the **power of compounding** in their account.

I want to explain how you can find at least $250 a month to invest from a different perspective. If we are going to spend all of our income, we need to adopt a "spending plan" with the $250 a month for investment included in it. Otherwise, we won't accumulate $1,000,000. Even if we don't have 33 years, our $250 could grow to a significant sum.

A **Spending Plan** is a way to set priorities for our regular spending. We can accumulate $1 million to accomplish all that we want to do in life by using just 10 percent of that income to buy assets that "grow by themselves."

Using a Spending Plan is **like brushing your teeth**—it's a habit that isn't that difficult to learn—then it is automatic. If we want our plan to become a habit, we have to practice it. If we consciously spend our income on those items on our priority list, we can't fail to develop the habit. We are teaching ourselves that we can have whatever we want in time. We are not saying "no" to that desire. We are saying put it on our list. We will get what we want eventually.

First, our Spending Plan must include what we need to function. Our future is part of our immediate needs in the sense that if we don't prepare now, we won't have the future we want. Again, building a $1,000,000 account is a lifelong process and requires making a commitment. Like building a business, it takes planning and following the steps we talked about so far.

There are a number of ways to identify the $250 a month we need to build our future. Some investors include the $250 in their automatic bill payment or have the trustee debit their account automatically. The contribution is just another bill like rent, mortgage, utilities, car payment, cable, phone, etc. They live on the balance of their income.

Others set up family goals and decide to put a certain amount in a separate account for each goal. In this way, they keep the wealth building process in the forefront of their monthly bill payments ritual.

Whatever way works for you. The important thing is to change the status of wealth building from a vague future desire to a monthly habit. "Set it and forget it" is the theme of investing.

Most people find that the easiest way is to set up an automatic debit of their checking account by the trustee at the time of the application for the Roth IRA. If we are using a Roth 401k or other employer account, we set up the retirement account with automatic contributions.

The Spending Plan idea works for all types of goals: college fund, emergency fund, vacation fund, new used car fund, business start-up fund, whatever we decide to put at the top of our list of priorities. If we don't have this list, we can make one easily.

Clients who are successful have made written plans in some form or other. They have some idea of how much they will need at some time in the future. For short-term goals we can use our savings account but for long-term goals we need to use higher return securities. Many clients have trouble deciding which investment to use for each goal.

I explain the chart we displayed on page 12 above. Stock mutual funds are the investment of choice for any long-term accumulation goal. As per the chart, annual returns of 10-12% are the norm for any accumulation over 10-15 years. Once we build up a sizable balance in a long-term account, we can "borrow" from ourselves for short-term needs as long as we pay ourselves back.

Thus, clients have used their long-term accumulation account for vacations, cars, appliances, emergencies, etc. This works if they pay themselves back. The account is set up as a Roth IRA so the *contributions* are not taxed when used before age 59.5. After that age, there are no taxes at all—NEVER. However, to meet our long-term goals, we have to pay ourselves back quickly to let our money keep working for us.

Another benefit of using a Spending Plan is that we become focused on how we spend our money. We are more inclined to buy only what we need. For most of us, when we go grocery shopping, we seek to get the most for our money by shopping for discounts and by buying in bulk. In the last ten years, the financial services industry has started to offer better values on products. We can avoid overpaying Wall Street firms and avoid buying products we really don't need.

How do we know? ***The Insiders Guides*** compiled by Dan Keppel provide an easy way to save $3,000 or more on financial products we already use. There are buyer's guides for each specific area. We review some of the ways to find $250 a month in savings in the next chapter.

We can't build wealth by spending more than we earn. Building wealth takes patience and commitment to contributing to our investment business every month. Some people don't try to be disciplined investors. They let the fund trustee debit the $250 or 10% every month so they can't fail to become a millionaire.

Are you paying too much?

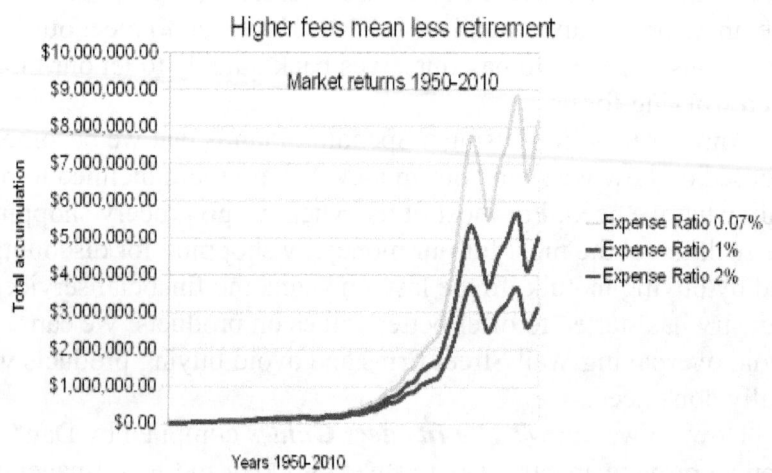

Higher fees mean less retirement

Market returns 1950-2010

Total accumulation

$10,000,000.00
$9,000,000.00
$8,000,000.00
$7,000,000.00
$6,000,000.00
$5,000,000.00
$4,000,000.00
$3,000,000.00
$2,000,000.00
$1,000,000.00
$0.00

Years 1950-2010

Expense Ratio 0.07%
Expense Ratio 1%
Expense Ratio 2%

8

Are their financial products efficient?

Any advisor can promise asset growth—BUT at what cost. It is easy to build wealth if we already have a pile of money. It takes 7-9 years to accumulate $1 million if you already have $500,000. Check the chart.

Monthly	Accumulation at 12% per year									
	5	10	15	20	25	30	35	40	45	50
$100	$8,167	$23,004	$49,958	$98,925	$187,884	$349,496	$643,095	$1,176,477	$2,145,469	$3,905,834
$200	$16,334	$46,008	$99,916	$197,850	$375,768	$698,992	$1,286,190	$2,352,954	$4,290,938	$7,811,668
$300	$24,501	$69,012	$149,874	$296,775	$563,652	$1,048,488	$1,929,285	$3,529,431	$6,436,408	$11,717,502
$500	$40,835	$115,020	$249,790	$494,625	$939,420	$1,747,480	$3,215,475	$5,882,385	$10,727,346	$19,529,169

But how do we capture that first $500,000, that $250,000, or even that first $50,000? It comes from buying assets that 'grow by themselves.' It takes time and the easiest way to make sure we reach our goal is to make our monthly contributions automatic.

But where do we get the $250 a month? The best way is to "REDIRECT" the **cash we already spend** on things we really don't need or can buy for less.

I think most working people waste $3,000 or more each year on finahcial services. They can stop paying for services they don't need. This takes the same type of questioning we go through when buying any commodity. When we buy groceries, do we buy the house brand or the one on sale or the one we see advertised?

In buying insurance or mutual funds, do we do research, compare costs and buy value? Do we pay an extra $1000 to buy the one the sales person is highlighting? The difference between paying full price for a new car and a 3-year-old model can be 40% or more. When we put our future on top of our priority list, we can REDIRECT the savings to a more worthwhile purpose. This is how millionaires become and stay millionaires.

It is the same with financial services. Most of us are not used to shopping for insurance, mutual funds, banking and mortgages. So we don't. We are operating under the mythology of Wall Street —'professionals' say we need them to help guide us, for a price. But you don't need us anymore. The world has changed.

Let's take some examples of **annual savings**:

Auto insurance: save $400 or more EVERY year by changing/dropping some benefits we don't need.

Home insurance: save $200 or more EVERY year by changing one limit.

Life insurance: save $1,000 or more EVERY year by using direct to consumer insurer.

Mutual funds: save $2-3,000 EVERY year by using low-cost providers.

Bank: save $120 EVERY year by using a low-cost provider of the benefits we usually use.

Mortgage: save $2,000 on closings and lower interest rates.

Investments: earn 15-30% guaranteed just by paying off credit cards.

Tax refund: Averages $3,022 a year and usually spent.

Using the Insiders' Guides put together by Dan Keppel in his book ***The Insiders' Guides to Buying Discount Financial Services: Buy Direct and Save $3,000 Every Year,*** we can REDIRECT the $250 a month without having to give up anything. We don't need to tighten our belt or make a budget. We can give up things we would not benefit from anyway.

Dan gave me a number of testimonials from people who have told him about their experience using the Guides.

George B. New York:
"I saved $1,356 on my vehicle insurance using your Insider's Guide to Vehicle Insurance. I saved by using some of your Insiders' 'tricks of the trade' like dropping the extras that I already had."
John D. New York:
"I canceled my life insurance and used the money to buy the mutual funds. You were right. I didn't need the insurance anymore. My kids are all grown. My new wife and I invest as much as we can now. Your Guide to 'Living' Insurance is a great way to look at our insurance needs."

Mark K. Ohio:

"I had no idea how to invest in the 401k that my new job offered. I have not been disappointed with the mutual funds suggested by other members. I saved about a $1,000 by transferring my old 401k mutual funds to the low-cost funds in your Guide. When I sold my primary residence in 2004, I followed members' advice with the gains. I use all your Guides to help me save more for my retirement since I got a late start. Thanks."

Dan has a great example of the big savings we can expect by shopping for insurance. Dan found that people usually pick name brands instead of shopping for services they need. Companies spend a lot for TV advertising and gimmicks.

Example:

MetLife charged $983 for a $300,000 30-year **term policy**. This same $300,000 benefit was sold by Savings Bank Life Insurance for $384 a year. Their financial strength ratings are A+ and their underwriting requirements are the same. The difference, $599, over 30 years is $17,970. If invested, this difference can add $175,000 to OUR **account**.

Most people are amazed at the difference a little research and shopping can accomplish. Even if we did not have Dan's Guide, a search of the Internet would reveal several portals that quote rates. Unfortunately, most people don't take the time to shop or don't know exactly what they need. The Guides help us make the decision of where to shop and what to buy.

Buy financial products like you buy "groceries not perfume" is the advice of value investor Benjamin Graham. Buying only what we need in every financial service area will provide the cash for contributions. **We give up nothing and gain our future**. Taking the time to shop in each area of our expenses helps us make our future happen. Shopping for an hour can add $175,000 to our account. Yes, it is worth it!

This strategy—to cut out the middle people who are taking your money with little benefit to you *over time*—makes sense and works!

The Roth IRA Rules

Contributions:

$5,500 ($6,500 over age 50) each year
Income under $128,000 (2013) single
married $188,000 (2013)

Distributions:

Tax-FREE for contributions.
And Tax-FREE for earnings if
Over age 591/2,
Account open 5 years,
Taxable earnings unless
Disabled,
First home ($10,000),
Death

Bonus:

Account can grow tax-FREE for life
Minimum distribution rules don't apply
Heirs don't pay income tax
Account has no maximum

Check with your tax preparer
www.IRS.gov/pub/irs-pdf/p590.pdf

9

How often do they change investments?

"We continue to make more money when *snoring*
than when active."

Warren Buffett, Berkshirehathaway.com/

This is the advice of the most successful investor of our day. He is
making it clear that we should NOT touch our investments very
often. Contrary to the advice of the Wall Street 'professionals,' he
leaves his assets alone to compound over time. He does not follow
the 'hot' investment of the day. He buys the stocks of growing
companies. He has held some investments for over 40 years.

Our emotions tell us to sell when our account balance goes
down. We want to buy the next big investment to make up for
previous losses. This is why we have a hard time following
Buffett's advice. However, the emotions that cause us to be bad
investors are what we can control—not the stock price of growing
companies worldwide.

Our contributions to our **account** need to be automatic so we
buy more shares when the market is down and less when it is up.
This helps us control our emotions. When the market is down, we
need to look at the line graph on page 16. We don't know when the
market will be up or down but we see that if we sell, we may miss
the next advance. This is why we have to remember Warren
Buffett's advice and hold on to stocks/stock funds. In fact, Mr
Buffett says "**our favorite holding period is forever.**"
http://www.berkshirehathaway.com/letters/1988.html

When we own a broad cross-section of the market, we really
don't have to worry about buying and selling our investments.
There is no better preparation for the long term. Besides, what
would we buy if we sold? Bank CD at 1-2%? We have seen that
stocks are the safest investment for periods over 10 years.

From my experience, there is only one way to avoid bad
investment decisions: Do NOT make any investment decisions in

haste. Stick with the idea that we only have to look at our tax-FREE account once a year. At that time, I make sure I am making contributions to the specific mutual fund I need to build in order to keep them equally balanced. That is the simplest way.

For instance, when I first started investing, I used the 500 Index. After I had accumulated enough to buy the Extended Market, I sold shares of the 500 Index ($3,000) and bought it. I kept investing into the 500 Index until I had the minimum for the next one on the list. I repeated this pattern until I had the minimum in each. Then I picked one to add $250 a month for one year. The next year, I did the same until I completed the list again and again.

Today, I am still making contributions using the same rotation but in my Roth 401k and Vanguard brokerage account. My wife does too. Once a year, I compare the account balances. I note what happened during the year for any one fund. I go to the Vanguard site and read about that fund. Do I need to make a change? No, usually I don't. I use the 10 funds listed above. They have done well consistently over the years. I buy other securities over time.

Notice that when we buy each fund at first, we have to sell shares in the 500 Index to do so. Because we are using a Roth IRA, there is no tax on this sale if the share price has gone up. Also, each year, our dividends are re-invested without paying tax on that income. This is part of the **miracle of compounding**. Our account is growing without taxes each year. Any other non-retirement account would be diminished by the tax and fee paid each year.

There is no need to sell funds that have done well in order to re-balance the 10 funds' balances equally. Most of the research shows that re-balancing each year does not change the long-term outcome of the whole portfolio. Some clients use their contributions each year to add to the fund that has grown the least. However, as each fund becomes larger, the effect of adding contributions becomes smaller over time.

When we have to sell shares to meet an emergency or avoid interest payments by using cash for large ticket items, we may sell shares in each fund by equal dollar amounts. This is a better strategy than selling shares in only one fund since we don't know which fund may recover the fastest going forward. In the same way as accumulating shares, we need to reimburse our accounts for the amounts used. It is very desirable to also continue to make contributions. This way we are assured of catching up to our position as we reach our goal.

However, we found that after accumulating a large proportion of our goal, adding the $250 per month did not seem to matter to the outcome. For instance, our client whose account is shown on page 22 took $25,000 for a used luxury car in the year the account hit over half a million. He also stopped making contributions. His account total did not suffer long term.

Actually this client redirected his $250 monthly contribution to his grandchild's Roth IRA **account** so that they might have a financial foundation all their life. If he keeps giving this $3,000 a year to his offspring for 40 years, they could have $2,000,000 by age 50. The grandchild "earns" $3,000 a year doing odd jobs for him. Learn more about this "Gift of a Lifetime" in Dan Keppel's book, amazon.com/Give-your-Grandchild-000-Lifetime/.

Manage investments once a year is wise advice. Our tax-FREE account does not require us to hire an advisor to manage it. Advisors do not know what the future holds anymore than we do so paying them 1-3% each year just reduces our annual returns. Their fees/charges can take up to 40% of our total accumulations over time.

We are investing for the long term and there is no proof that switching from one fund or stock to another during the year does anything to help our results. As we add more contributions, we can rotate through each fund we use. The less we tamper with our account the better. The *Miracle of Compounding* only works when we do NOT "manage" our money.

Your Action Plan

This week:
Goal

_____

_____

This month:
Goal

_____

_____

_____

_____

This year:
Goals

_____

_____

_____

_____

_____

_____

_____

_____

_____

_____

_____

_____

_____

_____

10

Do they help you plan purchases and retirement?

We have used the 10 funds to build wealth. We have learned to be patient and accumulate $1,000,000 or more. We have paid back any amounts that we borrowed to pay cash for large purchases. We have been fortunate that the historical averages of market returns have produced the accumulations we set as our goals.

NOW WHAT?

Now we can take 8% out of the account each year and pay no income taxes. As of 2013, most states follow the IRS code on our **account**, a Roth IRA—§ 408 trust account.
http://www.irs.gov/retirement/article/0,,id=137307,00.html

Some clients have moved some of their accumulations into a bond fund in order to provide a monthly check to their checking account for their regular expenses. They created a retirement spending plan that assured them of that monthly income of a fixed dollar amount with this Guide. amazon.com/Your-Retirement-Spending-Plan-enough

We have to create our $1,000,000 nest egg in order to provide the same buying power as we have today because of inflation. I am assuming that most working families will need at least $50,000 a year to live on in retirement. We don't know what will happen to Social Security by 2033. We don't know what employer pensions might look like by then. I am assuming that inflation will continue at a 3% rate. It might be more or less. I have no idea. However, we must prepare for inflation. Planning is crucial to success.

At 3%, inflation will make the goods we buy now for $50,000 cost about $80,000. This is not exact. I don't know what will happen in 40 days let alone 40 years. If Social Security or employer pensions can add to our basic income, that is fine. But we don't want to count on them.

I am using $50,000 as a basic-needs income because that has been my experience of what working people desire. It is also an amount that could be generated by our $1,000,000 account balance.

Many clients use 6-8% as a target for their investment returns in retirement. This is just an approximation of the average returns over time. In lean years, they take out less.

Some clients move half their balances into a bond or balanced fund in order to generate the income for the coming year. The balance of their account remains in the broad stock funds we have listed above. These funds will continue to produce returns in the 10-12% range. If there is a bad year like 2008, we are not taking money out of our principal at a bad time. We take the money from a bond fund like the Vanguard Total Bond which has traditionally been less volatile.

The funds we have listed above include some of the most consistent low volatility returns over time. The Wellesley Income fund has produced over 10% per year on average since 1970. It contains stocks and bonds. **This fund alone might be our source** of annual withdrawals of principal and dividends. Since this account is not taxable, there are no tax considerations in the decision of which fund to tap for our monthly income.

Because we have no tax liability on this income of $80,000 per year, we may not have to pay tax on our other income like Social Security and/or our qualified retirement funds. 85% of Social Security benefits are currently subject to federal income taxes. The IRS worksheet determines the percentage based on all our other income. Typically those with little or no other income currently have no tax due on their Social Security benefits. Pensions are taxed as income since we did not pay tax on the contributions.

In most cases, we will pay little income tax on our income in retirement since the bulk of it, $80,000 ($50,000 adjusted for inflation), will be tax-FREE. This will give us up to 30% more cash to spend compared with others who do not have this account. Pensions and other taxable income may be taxed at even higher rates in the future to pay for the two wars and two tax cuts that we endured since 2001. We have never gone to war and taken tax breaks at the same time before so this will take time to work out.

Our tax-FREE income will provide us with our basic-needs income and if we continue to follow the same 10 steps of building wealth, we will find a comfortable lifestyle throughout the 30 to 40 years of not working unless we want to.

I and many clients are assuming we will work at least part time after we take full retirement and begin collecting Social Security. If benefits are cut, we will need to work. We are encouraged to use our tax-FREE income to develop a small business since this can help us control the income that is taxed.

As I mentioned at the beginning of this book, many working millionaires are self-employed. Running a small business is a great way to control the taxes they pay. Taxes are the biggest killer of wealth building that exists. It destroys the compounding factor.

The accumulation of $1,000,000 over time can be achieved with patience and perseverance. Spending the income that $1,000,000 can generate may require us to take some principal from time to time. If we use the same 10 steps of wealth building to do this, we will probably have enough to take care of long-term health care and other unforeseen expenses. Since we don't know what may happen, we will want to continue the same habits we have developed before retirement. We live within our means.

We may find that we will have a sizable legacy as we age. There are many ways to pass on our wealth that don't require an attorney on contingency or complicated legal formulations. Many clients have found that incremental gifts to charity and family provide immediate gratification. They have used the suggestions for wealth transfer Dan Keppel presented in the *Retirement Spending Plan*.

Plan purchases and retirement spending wisely. Planning assures that our retirement income is tax-FREE and has the purchasing power of about $50,000 in today's dollars. Working millionaires typically don't go out and buy a mansion and the trappings of the wealthy when they retire. They usually have paid off their homes. They travel and share with family. Some continue to earn income doing what they enjoy or provide help to others in their volunteer efforts. This is your life when you become a *tax-FREE millionaire.*

The Keys to Wealth

1. **Costs matter**: Broker/advisor cost 1% to 3% every year

   If you use a salesperson, costs take HALF your money!
   $3,000 per year @11%   for 33 years = $1,018,177
   $3,000 per year @11-1% for 33 years = $778,768
   $3,000 per year @11-2% for 33 years = $613,805
   $3,000 per year @11-3% for 33 years = $486,634
   www.moneychimp.com/calculator/compound_interest_calculator.htm

2. Broker/advisor stock-picking does not beat index funds over time. No money manager has been able to beat the markets consistently. No one can forecast the future. online.wsj.com/article/ SB10001424127887324059704578471154109438438.html

3. **Compounding** creates investment success. The chance of you buying AND selling, both, at the right times, is near zero. Warren Buffett's holding period is "forever."

4. A **tax-FREE** investment account increases your balance 30%.

5. Putting all your money in one stock or market sector guarantees failure over time. No one investment is perfect. Buy a **group of growing global businesses.**

6. '**Dollar cost average**' buying technique lowers the cost of shares over time. When you invest a fixed amount each month, you buy more mutual fund shares when the price is low and less when high. Over time, you will own more shares at a lower average cost.

7. **Consistency** wins over the long term. Quick in and out trading only benefits Wall Street. Market timing may work for a short time but the odds of being right on the buy and sell are long.

8. **Patience** is required to allow your money to work for you. Building a business takes time. Investing is betting to most of us.

Conclusion

Do you really need these guys?

Invest $9 a day, $3,000 a year for $1,000,000 over time.

Most wealthy people have learned to use these strategies already. That is what allowed them to accumulate over $1,000,000. Some have asked for help. Some used the 10 Vanguard funds. They did not need stock-picking skills. They did not need to use individual stocks or high-cost mutual funds offered by our salespeople. I personally use many Vanguard and Fidelity funds.

Many of these folks had done research on their own and really just needed confirmation of their own thinking. They made the decisions but wanted to be sure there was nothing they were missing. The industry has made building wealth a mystery so that they could tell us we need them—a "doctor" of financial health who we paid very well. The industry takes $560 billions from investors' accounts year after year with limited improvement. Trading stocks usually does NOT benefit us.
pbs.org/moyers/journal/09282007/

A person paying 1% to 3% of their portfolio every year to an advisor can't then admit they get very little for their money. Most advisors can't beat the investment returns of the market so that $3-5,000 a year in fees is really just a drag on earnings. Over time that fee compounds as your balance goes up and can take up to 40% of your total possible accumulations. Advisors like to buy and sell creating taxes and fees. But these costs don't help us.

As Buffett said, **compounding is key** to reaching our money goals. If we pay 2% to get 10-12%, we net 8-10%. Since we know that no advisor can guarantee 10-12% and most studies show investing directly without a "professional" can yield the same result, there is no reason to give up 2%. Advisors usually charge 2% whether they beat the averages or not so it is better to go for the 10-12% on our own. **Advisors don't give refunds if they fail!**

The clear winning strategy is to use the 10 funds and let compounding work its magic. Over time using a tax-FREE account with low fees, we can accumulate $1,000,000 from $250 a month at 10-12%. Using a compounding calculator moneychimp.com/calculator/compound_interest_calculator.htm, we find the range is 31 to 35 years. If our spouse has an account, we can shorten the time to 26-29 years for a family $1 million.

If we use an advisor, we may give up over $300,000 of $1 million in total accumulation. Research has shown that the average brokerage investor actually earns **2.56%** not 10.38% annually. 1990-2010 (QAIB)DALBARinc.com.moneychimp.com/features/market_cagr.htm

Our 10 funds for building wealth work because they are low-cost strategies inside a unique **tax-FREE trust account.** This eliminates the biggest killers of wealth: TAXES and FEES. We learned that compounding over time is the real engine for building wealth. Most people are NOT going to be successful at this because they have no patience to let compounding do the work.

We can be our own masters of tax-FREE wealth with patience. There is no need to pick stocks or hire expensive advisors or product pushers with hidden fees. We can do it ourselves as long as we have a plan. The plan is the following 10 steps:

1. Avoid taxes with a tax-advantaged trust account.
2. Use a lifetime investment plan.
3. Compound high earnings over time.
4. Make investing automatic.
5. Avoid high-cost investment products.
6. Buy assets that grow in any economy.
7. Invest at least 10% of income.
8. Buy financial products like you buy groceries not perfume.
9. Manage investments once a year.
10. Plan purchases and retirement spending wisely.

You must take the first step. Advisors can't profit from these steps. You have to call Vanguard or TIAA-CREF *yourself* to set up your account. Advisors can't. It takes about an hour to set up a Roth IRA for each of you. You can do it online or by phone. You can begin with TIAA-CREF and $100 automatic contributions or Vanguard with $1,000. Put the contributions on automatic so you don't have to decide every month whether to invest. That is usually how people fail. Life happens and there is always an emergency that requires cash. But future life happens too and you want to be spending your $80,000 a year not praying Washington won't cut

Social Security benefits every year.

There is a clear reason why "working millionaires" become wealthy. It is not luck or inheritance. Millions of immigrants to this country have done it before. They lived below their means. They saved and invested in businesses. They did not let temporary cash flow problems stop them from building wealth. They used the same path to building wealth every day.

As many clients say, "I never even miss the contributions because I never see them. Then all of a sudden, I see my statement has $25,000, $50,000, $250,000, $1,000,000, $2,000,000. We are talking real money here."

That is the Miracle of Compounding—
The most important factor in building wealth.

You can do it too. Give it a try. You will be surprised how easy it becomes over time. Ignore Wall Street hype and earn more!

Tax-advantaged wealth is a *habit* not a lottery.

Call Vanguard 800 937-5544 or TIAA-CREF **800 842-2252** today.

Just do it! Thank me later.

NOTES

The Author

Ian Sender has been a financial services executive for over 25 years. He was a managing director of sales units of securities firms. He is one of the Insiders who contributed to the *The Insiders Guides* set of buyers' guides edited by Dan Keppel. Ian lives in New Jersey and the Caymans (taxes).

To receive Dan Keppel's weekly Alert, go to www.TheInsidersGuides.com